IPSWICH

IN OLD PHOTOGRAPHS

MEMBERS OF THE IPSWICH AND DISTRICT PHOTOGRAPHIC SOCIETY on a day trip to Pin Mill in 1933. Percy Chinery took this picture of fellow members at work focusing on a group of children sitting on a boat (right). With their backs to the camera are Mr W.C.S. Girling and his wife, whose work is included in this book. The two photographers are Mr Garling (left), and Mr Brook.

DEDICATION

To my wife Anne and son James for their patience when I come home with an old camera to restore, or yet another box of dusty old glass negatives. And to the 'good old days'.

IPSWICH

IN OLD PHOTOGRAPHS

COLLECTED BY

DAVID KINDRED

A Budding Book

First published in 1990 by Alan Sutton Publishing Limited

This edition published in 1999 by Budding Books,
an imprint of Sutton Publishing Limited
Phoenix Mill · Thrupp · Stroud · Gloucestershire GL5 2BU

A catalogue record for this book is available from the British Library

ISBN 1-84015-120-X

Typesetting and origination by
Sutton Publishing Limited.
Printed in Great Britain by
Redwood Books, Trowbridge, Wiltshire

INTRODUCTION

The photographs in this book capture life in Ipswich over the last hundred years, but what a pity it is that photography was not invented earlier. For Ipswich is a town with a history dating back thousands of years. The name goes back to Saxon times, when the settlement was known as Gipes-wic, meaning Gipi's (pronounced Yippy) Village. How wonderful, for instance, to see photographs of one of the town's best-known historical figures on the site of his planned college, only the gate of which survives in College Street – Cardinal Wolsey was born in Ipswich, the son of innkeeper and butcher, Robert Wolsey.

Royal visits now are always occasions when miles of film are exposed. How much would have been used if photography could have recorded the visit of Edward III on his way through Ipswich to Walton in 1339 when he confirmed the charter which his predecessors had granted to Ipswich? The chapel in Lady Lane was visited by Queen Katherine of Aragon in 1517 and Henry VIII in 1522. James II and his brother, Charles II, both visited in the seventeenth century, and William III in 1693. Many similar historic occasions are recorded but not, of course, by photographs. The camera existed; it was a light-sensitive film and fixable image that eluded the pioneers of photography.

The camera obscura was a device used to help artists sketch scenes. It was a light-tight box with a lens at one end and a ground glass screen at the other, on which the artist could trace the scene. It had been in use for hundreds of years before a means of recording the image was invented in the 1830s. Frenchman Louis Daguerre was the first to patent a practical form of photography, in 1839,

A TEAM OF SUGAR BEET PICKERS captured by the Titshall Brothers at work on the outskirts of town *c*. 1928.

with an image on silver plate known as the daguerreotype. Working in England at the same time, William Henry Fox-Talbot was making paper negatives and prints similar to the photography of today. The oldest photographs I have seen of Ipswich are a daguerreotype of the Cornhill in 1859, and the work of local artist and photographer, Robert Burrows, or local philanthropist, Richard Dykes Alexander, of the late 1850s and 1860s.

The paper negative system of Fox-Talbot was updated when it was found how to make the photographic chemicals adhere to glass. From the 1840s until the 1870s photographers had to make their own plates at the scene, take the picture and develop it before it was dry, as it was only sensitive to light while it was still wet. A portable darkroom was necessarily taken everywhere with the photographer. Thousands of wet-plate portrait photographs by Ipswich photographers have survived. The Victorian fashion for photography, headed by Queen Victoria, led to as many as fifteen photographers working in Ipswich in the Victorian period, but because of the difficulty of working with wet-plate photography few left their studio.

William Vick ran a studio at the junction of London Road and Clarkson Street for thirty years until he retired in 1897. He was keen to record the history of the town, and published a book and boxed sets of photographs of 'Ipswich Past and Present'. The daguerreotype of the Cornhill only survives as an image because Vick copied the original for his pictures of old Ipswich. Some of William Vick's work is included in this book, with his picture of the dock from Stoke Bridge on the cover. William Vick's pictures still turn up. I bought a set of his work at a collectors' fair at Copdock in 1989.

During the 1870s dry plates were perfected, photographers became more mobile, and amateur photography became more practical. I include some of the work of local amateur John 'Herbert' Gooding who took pictures in the town at the turn of the century.

The production of postcard pictures and a very regular postal delivery meant a message could be sent across town within a few hours. This fact, together with the trend to send cards home from holiday, meant that the photographer could sell his work as postcard views. Everything was photographed; disasters, rows of houses, street scenes, and big events were all produced as postcards. Some were real photographs printed by the dozen; others were reproduced in their thousands. The major period of postcard photography is from about 1890 to 1920.

The work of Ipswich photographers, the Titshall Brothers, who had a studio in Spring Road, is a unique record of working life in the area. They took pictures with their half-plate wooden camera of people at work such as dustmen, road builders and dockers. Their work has survived thanks to a friend of theirs, Doug Cotton of Camberley Road. Mr Cotton took the glass negatives home in the 1950s when the brothers were planning to dump them and although Mr Cotton has no photographic knowledge he salvaged as many of the plates, which had got damp through bad storage, as possible. I am forever grateful to Mr Cotton for giving me access to the pictures of Ipswich at work in the 1920s and '30s.

With the help of postcard collectors, the work of Ipswich Photographic Society member, Mr W.C.S. Girling of Powling Road, Ipswich, Mr John Gooding of Sproughton, who gave me his uncle's glass negatives, the family of the late Mr Ernie Howard who loaned me his work from the early years of this century, and

Ralph Chinery who gave me his father's work from the 1930s, I have gathered some more unusual pictures of Ipswich from 1859 to the changes in the town of the mid-1960s.

The pictures are, where possible, grouped in themes, such as buses, the war years, bakers, dairymen or the dock, but some pictures fall into several categories. Trams and trolleybuses, for instance, feature often in street scenes outside their own category.

The dating of pictures can be difficult. Some are marked with the exact date or year they were taken, others have to be an informed guess based on clues in the picture. Where this is the case I have given the date as approximate. If any two 'experts' see an old picture, however, they will find some point of detail to disagree upon.

I hope you enjoy this book of Ipswich in the past.

David Kindred, 1990

AN EARLY EXAMPLE OF PHOTOGRAPHY IN IPSWICH showing Westgate Street from the Cornhill in 1859. The original was taken as a daguerreotype by Mr W. Thompson, who loaned the picture to William Vick to copy for his sets of prints showing Ipswich 'Past and Present'. Most of this scene has gone. The frontage of the old Crown and Anchor hotel is the only surviving building. The American Stores was demolished in the late 1870s to widen the road. This corner is now Grimwade's shop.

PAGES 9 TO 14 INCLUDE PICTURES BY WILLIAM VICK from his set of Victorian Ipswich. Above, a view from the Town Hall, newly completed in 1868, of Tavern Street. Included in the view are St Mary-Le-Tower and St Lawrence Churches. The shop with the target on the roof was F.A. Bales, Gunsmiths, now Lloyds buildings. The central area of this scene is now dominated by the Tower Ramparts shopping centre.

WATERLOO HOUSE ON THE CORNHILL c. 1885. The archway was the entrance to Mumfords Passage, named after Dr Mumford who lived at the top of the lane at Tower Ramparts.

THE POST OFFICE BUILDING at the junction of Princes Street and the Buttermarket was built in 1856/7 as a private enterprise, the fifth site for the service. It was replaced by the present Cornhill office, built 1879/80.

THE MUSEUM WHEN IT WAS IN MUSEUM STREET. In 1846 the town hired the rooms to house some of the town's treasures. The building became a ballroom when the museum moved to High Street in 1881.

BURLINGTON CHAPEL IN LONDON ROAD, *c.* 1880.

TOWER RAMPARTS, part of the town's defences, originally built in 1203. It is photographed *c.* 1875 when the line of the town bank was clear. The view is from the top of Providence Street looking towards the present bus station.

TOWER RAMPARTS c. 1890. Electric House now stands where the two houses in the middle distance stand. The left side of this view is now the Tower Ramparts shopping centre.

A SIMILAR VIEW TO THE PICTURE ABOVE, taken in 1968. The chimney of the William Pretty clothing factory, demolished in the 1980s, can be seen in both pictures. On the left is the Tower Ramparts School.

A VIEW OF THE RIVER ORWELL c. 1888. A boy and girl play with a spade opposite the Ancaster Road rail bridge. In the distance is the Station Hotel.

THE DUKE STREET ROUNDABOUT now dominates this junction of Back Hamlet and Fore Street. This picture was taken in the late 1870s.

THE WORLD FAMOUS BARNUM AND BAILEY CIRCUS visited Ipswich in 1898 and in 1899. The circus arrived by special train and paraded through town. Thousands watched the shows on a site near Bramford Road. The parade is photographed in Fonnereau Road.

A BUSY CORNHILL *c.* 1910 from the window of Grimwade's shop.

CROWDS PACKED THE CORNHILL for the proclamation of King George V in 1910.

THE JUNCTION OF THE BUTTERMARKET AND PRINCES STREET *c.* 1910.

THE TOWN'S HORSE-DRAWN TRAMS ran from 1880 to 1903. This picture, taken from the Town Hall steps, shows the cabman's shelter which was removed to Christchurch Park in 1893 (see picture opposite). On the right, one of the trams makes its way down Princes Street to the station.

A VIEW OF THE CORNHILL in July 1900, taken by amateur photographer John 'Herbert' Gooding and featuring one of the horse-drawn trams and a line of cabs. The lamp and drinking trough for the horses was not removed until 1928.

THE CABMAN'S SHELTER on its way to Christchurch Park in 1895. Photographer Harry Walters captured the steamroller towing the shelter outside his studio in St Margarets Plain. The shelter now stands by the Bolton Lane gate in Christchurch Park.

MAINTENANCE MEN AT WORK on top of the Town Hall c. 1912.

TWO VIEWS OF QUEEN STREET. The top picture looks out of the street to the Corn Exchange *c.* 1920. The bottom picture, taken *c.* 1904, looks the other way. The row of shops on the right were demolished to widen the road.

CHURCHMANS, THE TOBACCONISTS at Hyde Park Corner *c.* 1880. The company established itself here in 1790 and moved to Portman Road in 1898. The town's old west gate, demolished in 1781, stood at the end of Westgate Street (right).

THE SAME VIEW in January 1956. The traffic control for this busy junction was by policeman on point duty. The two policemen in this picture are about to change shift.

A VIEW OF CARR STREET c. 1912 looking towards Majors Corner. The Lyceum Theatre (centre) was a red-brick building seating 1,100. The management ran live theatre until 1923, but reopened as a cinema following the summer recess. In 1936 the Lyceum was sold to Great Universal Stores who replaced it with a new shop. The Eastgate Shopping Centre is now on this site.

CARR STREET LOOKING TOWARDS WHITE HORSE CORNER. The distinctive tower on the front of the *East Anglian Daily Times* company offices was lost when the site was demolished in 1966 for redevelopment. The few buildings on the far right are all that remain.

CARR STREET IN THE EARLY MORNING SUNSHINE in 1888 by William Vick. This is the view from the Great White Horse Hotel.

A POLICEMAN ON DUTY AT WHITE HORSE CORNER. A tram, a horse-drawn buggy and an open-top car provide a good mix of traffic at the end of Carr Street c. 1908.

CARR STREET AT THE TURN OF THE CENTURY. The timber-framed building on the left was James Redstone's store selling fancy goods and toys. It was taken down in 1907 to clear the site for the new Ipswich Co-operative Society Store.

A GROUP OF CHILDREN WATCH THE PHOTOGRAPHER AT WORK in 1907 at the Corner of Cox Lane. They are standing next to the site cleared for the new Co-operative Society Store.

ALBERT LIST'S CYCLE SHOP IN CARR STREET c. 1912. At that time List had a shop on both sides of the street. A reflection of the opposite shop, selling prams, can be seen in the window. The manager at the door is Mr Stanley Girling.

TAVERN STREET FROM CARR STREET in January 1956.

THE GREAT WHITE HORSE HOTEL IN TAVERN STREET inside and out c. 1910.

S 2800 COURTYARD, GREAT WHITE HORSE HOTEL, IPSWICH

FREDERICK FISH AND SON'S STORE IN TAVERN STREET in 1924. The store was a 'Merchant Drapers and House Furnishers', even offering a funeral furnishing service. It became a branch of Boots the Chemists, and was demolished in the mid-1980s and rebuilt in a similar style. Below, an advertisement for the store of 1926.

FREDK. FISH & SON.

HOUSE FURNISHERS.

MERCHANT DRAPERS.

Suffolk House, Tavern St., Ipswich.

WESTGATE STREET from the junction of Museum Street looking towards the Cornhill in June 1897. The flags are flying to celebrate the Diamond Jubilee of Queen Victoria.

WESTGATE STREET in the 1950s. On the right is W.H. Smith's, stationer and bookseller, then a much smaller shop, and on the left cars are able to park with ease outside the Crown and Anchor Hotel.

THE CROWN AND ANCHOR IN THE 1870s by William Vick.

FOOTMAN, PRETTY & CO.,

Complete House Furnishers and General Drapers,

Established
1815.

New Furniture Showrooms
Just Opened.

ESTIMATES FOR REMOVALS FREE.

WATERLOO HOUSE, IPSWICH.

AN ADVERTISEMENT for Footman, Pretty and Company's Waterloo House store in Westgate Street from 1926, when the frontage of the business spanned from the Cornhill to Providence Street.

WESTGATE STREET from outside the Crown and Anchor c. 1910.

WESTGATE STREET from the junction of Museum Street in January 1956.

A VIEW FROM PRINCES STREET, c. 1890, of the Cattle Market which moved to here in 1856 from a town centre site still referred to as 'The Old Cattle Market'. It is now a bus station. The Sporting Farmer public house now stands roughly where this picture was taken.

DURING THE BOER WAR British troops were surrounded and besieged at Mafeking. The flags were out in Nacton Road in 1900 when news came through that the siege was over. John 'Herbert' Gooding, who lived in the house at the junction of Nacton Road, took this picture of the celebrations. The house is now converted to shops.

THE BOER WAR MEMORIAL being unveiled on the Cornhill 29 September 1903.

THE MEMORIAL OUTSIDE THE GOLDEN LION HOTEL. This fine statue of a soldier with his head bowed was removed to Christchurch Park in 1931.

THE FAMILY AND FRIENDS OF JOHN JEREMIAH GOODING, seen in the picture, at a picnic in the garden of his home in Nacton Road in July 1899. This was a very formal event, a long way from today's barbecue.

THE JUNCTION OF CLAPGATE LANE AND NACTON ROAD in the winter of 1900.

BISHOPS HILL, 1894.

THE RELEASE OF WOMAN'S FREEDOM LEAGUE MEMBER, Mrs Constance Andrews (seated centre) of No. 160 Norwich Road, on 27 May 1911. Miss Andrews had refused to pay a fine for keeping a dog without a licence, claiming that 'tax and representation ought to go together'. She was sentenced to seven days' prison, without hard labour, at the town prison (now the County Hall). The picture was taken in Grimwade Street as Miss Andrews was driven for a celebration breakfast.

MEMBERS OF THE BOROUGH RESERVE POLICE who served during the General Strike, May 1926, grouped on the Town Hall steps.

IPSWICH BOROUGH MOUNTED POLICE on the Cornhill during the general strike of 1926.

THE EMPRESS SKATING RINK at the junction of Portman Road and Portman Walk. The rink opened in July 1919, an event attended by thousands. The building was demolished in the 1960s after serving many years as J. Harvey Ltd's clothing factory.

HENRI SALMET with his Bleriot monoplane, the first aircraft to land in Ipswich, close to Stone Lodge Lane in August 1912. Thousands of people turned out to watch the event which was sponsored by the *Daily Mail* as part of a tour.

AT THE END OF THE FIRST WORLD WAR Ipswich erected a temporary memorial 'To the Fallen' at the junction of Princes Street and the Buttermarket.

THOUSANDS GATHERED ON THE CORNHILL on 6 July 1919 to celebrate Peace Day.

A PEACE TABLEAU in Kingston Road.

CELEBRATIONS OF PEACE at the Round Pond in Christchurch Park in July 1919 included a spectacular display of diving. Thousands gathered at the pond for a display arranged by the Ipswich Swimming Club. It is difficult to imagine such an event at the pond today.

CROWDS AT THE JUNCTION of Northgate Street and St Margarets Plain escort a pipe band. This event is not identified but could be part of the First World War peace day celebrations of July 1919. The picture was taken by photographer Harry Walters from the window of his studio on St Margarets Plain.

A GROUP OF INFANTS at St Mary's School, which was in Croft Street, pose for the camera in 1900.

BOYS OF ST MARY'S SCHOOL in 1900. How many of these innocent young faces survived the First World War?

SOME STERN FACES at Clifford Road School in the 1930s.

CROWDS GATHER IN ORWELL PLACE at the turn of the century. The event is not identified, but looks like a day for best clothes. The buildings on the left are long gone. St Pancras Church now stands behind the line of these buildings. The buildings on the right remain, with Martin and Newby's site on the far right. The timber-framed public house, the Spread Eagle, is in the centre background.

ORWELL PLACE FROM EAGLE STREET in 1906.

A GREAT EASTERN RAILWAY'S BUS at the station in 1914. The service ran to Shotley. It must have been a rough ride on the unmade road with the bus's solid tyres.

DISASTER HIT THE TOWN CENTRE on 6 April 1914 when the premises of R.D. and J.B. Fraser and other buildings in Princes Street were destroyed by fire. The efficiency of the town's fire service was brought into question by the blaze which razed the buildings to the ground. There were calls to get rid of the horse-drawn machines and buy a modern motor fire-engine, not regarded as entirely reliable in those days. The council compromised and bought a Shand Mason 'First turn out' machine with a 50 ft ladder and a nozzle fitted at the top. Ipswich did not get its first motor fire-engine until 1918, and it was 1920 before the horses were finally paid off. The town council formed its own fire brigade in 1875. The fire-engine station was in Waterworks Street, moving to Bond Street on 13 November 1899, and from there to Colchester Road in the early 1960s.

FIREMEN IN BRASS HELMETS tackle the Fraser's fire from Elm Street. In the background is the Corn Exchange.

THE SCENE AFTER FRASER'S FIRE.

A FIRE-DAMAGED PART of E.R. and F. Turner Ltd's Greyfriars Foundry in 1911. The photographer has taken his picture as another cameraman is setting up his wooden camera and tripod.

THE RAIL LINE FROM COLCHESTER TO IPSWICH, completing the connection with London, saw its first train in June 1846 to a station south of the present tunnel. Station Street is still with us although the station moved from there to its present site in 1860. The old station became the site of the locomotive power depot known to railwaymen as 'Ipswich Loco'. The picture above is of the first passenger engine to make the run from Ipswich to Felixstowe in May 1877. It was named *Tomline* after George Tomline, the owner of Orwell Park, Nacton, who financed the line to Felixstowe from Westerfield Junction.

A CLAUDE HAMILTON CLASS EXPRESS at 'Ipswich Loco' in the 1930s with a crew of fitters and cleaners during their tea break.

A BREAK IN THE WORK for a photo by the Titshall Brothers at 'Ipswich Loco'.

TO CELEBRATE THE SILVER JUBILEE of King George V Monday 6 May 1935 was a holiday. By 9 o'clock, the *Evening Star* reported, every inch of space on the Cornhill was taken. At 10 o'clock a procession formed up at Barrack Corner to move through the town. Mounted police led the fire brigade through Westgate Street. This picture was taken by Mr W.C.S. Girling, a member of the Ipswich and District Photographic Society.

CROWDS GATHER AT BARRACK CORNER waiting for the start of the procession. The entrance to Clarkson Street is in the centre of the picture.

THE PROCESSION, led by an elephant, crosses the Cornhill.

MR W.C.S. GIRLING'S PICTURE of St Matthews Street on 6 May 1935 as the town celebrates the Silver Jubilee of King George V. On the right of the picture is the entrance to Berners Street.

A VICTORIAN VIEW of the junction of Princes Street and Friars Street with the premises of George King, saddle and harness maker, and below, the same scene *c.* 1910 with the building of Grimwade Ridley, wholesale druggist, in the centre. This site is now occupied by the glass-faced building of Willis Faber.

A 1912 VIEW OF THE ANCIENT HOUSE in the Buttermarket, with a splendid car parked outside, facing the opposite way to the present one-way system.

THE BUTTERMARKET from Upper Brook Street in the late 1920s. Bernard Hines sports shop, one of the first to specialize in sports wear, is on the left.

THIS HUGE STATUE OF QUEEN VICTORIA was unveiled in May 1904. It was removed during the Second World War and melted down for munitions.

A PICTURE TAKEN in the children's ward of the old Ipswich and East Suffolk Hospital, in Anglesea Road, of a fund-raising scheme to endow a cot for £500. The notice says, 'Verily I say unto you, in as much as ye have done it unto one of the least of these, my little sick ones, ye have done it unto me'. Signed J. Moss, Head Porter.

A THREADBARE FAMILY GROUP photographed by the Ipswich photographers, the Titshall Brothers.

A GROUP IN KELLY ROAD in 1927 looks like something from one of Charles Dickens' stories imposed upon a modern background. The children on the donkey cart were the sons and nephew of the pipe-smoking Ben Gooderum. They are (left to right) John, (William in the floppy hat), George, and cousin Freddie Pugh. Father Ben, who had been in the Royal Artillery, then worked for Ransomes and Rapier, kept the cart for pleasure. The picture was taken outside the newly-built council houses.

TRANSPORT ACCIDENTS are as old as the wheel. On these two pages we look at three incidents on the town's roads. Above, a car hit the window of Green and Hatfield's antique shop at the corner of Northgate Street and St Margarets Plain on 5 June 1918, causing damage to the china etc. worth £80, and £35 to the window. This is another picture from the first floor window of Harry Walter's studio (see page 43). Above right, a traction engine slips over near Stoke Bridge in the early years of the century and, below right, an overturned MG 18/80 in the summer of 1934. Percy Chinery took this picture from the window of his home in London Road.

WOODBRIDGE ROAD from the top of Warwick Road *c.* 1905.

A TRIAL RUN for the new electric trams which replaced the horse-drawn trams in November 1903. This picture was taken at the corner of Kitchener Road and Norwich Road.

THREE OF THE TOWN'S ELECTRIC TRAMS at the junction of Cauldwell Hall Road and St John's Road.

SIX TRAMS UNLOAD what looks like a children's outing on a rainy day.

A TRAIN AND TRAM MEET at the Norwich Road bridge. A picture taken from the end of what is now Dales Road looking out of town.

THE END OF THE LINE for the trams as they are dismantled in Norwich Road on 27 July 1926.

THE TROLLEYBUS had started to replace the trams by the late summer of 1923. This picture of bus No. 3 in Princes Street in 1924 also shows the tram lines being removed.

A SINGLE DECK TROLLEYBUS and a diesel bus together in Lloyds Avenue.

A PAIR OF TROLLEYBUSES pass at the bottom of Bishops Hill in the late 1940s.

A TROLLEYBUS IN FORE HAMLET in the late 1940s passes a line of half-demolished houses.

IPSWICH ENGINEERING COMPANY, Ransomes Sims and Jefferies, built some of the town's trolleybuses. Officials of the company and the Corporation Transport Department are pictured at the hand over of one of the trams just prior to the Royal Show (see facing page). Mr Hampton Blackstone (third right), was the manager of Ipswich Corporation buses.

THE ROYAL SHOW CAME TO IPSWICH in 1934. It was held on open ground at the top of Crane Hill, on the London Road – now Chantry – housing estate. Thousands travelled to the event by a special trolleybus service. Queues of buses pulled slowly up the hill, overloading the electrical system at the power station in Constantine Road, where workers had to hold in the circuit breakers to keep the current running. Between 3 and 7 July, the period of the show, passenger receipts totalled £3,260, the buses covered 45,134 miles and carried 396,294 passengers. The top picture by Mr W.C.S. Girling, and the one below by Mr Percy Chinery, are both of buses serving the Royal Show.

THE ROYAL SHOW CAR PARK at Chantry. It was a rare sight in those days to see so many cars together. Both pictures are by Mr W.C.S. Girling.

SOME OF THE MEN who built the sugar beet factory in Sproughton Road take a break c. 1930.

THE PLOUGH public house and the Old Cattle Market bus station in 1948.

THE WINDMILL AT STOKE stood on the hill behind the railway station. It was the last of the mills close to the town to grind corn. The last miller was Mr William Goodchild (on the right of the picture) who worked the mill until 1884. It was dismantled in 1887. Mr Goodchild thought that as housing in the area increased so the wind to the mill decreased, slowly putting the mill out of business.

THIS GROUP OF MEDIEVAL HOUSES at the corner of Silent Street and St Nicholas Street are reputed to be the birthplace of Cardinal Wolsey. The postcard above shows a tram passing by c. 1910. The photograph by Percy Chinery shows how by the 1930s the plaster coat had been removed and the timbers exposed.

THIS LINE OF SHOPS in St Peters Street has changed little since this picture of around 1908.

THE HALF MOON INN, at the corner of Lower Brook Street and Foundation Street, was demolished soon after this 1959 picture. A warehouse stood on the site until stylish offices were built in 1989.

THESE TWO VIEWS OF NORWICH ROAD from the end of Orford Street, taken at the turn of the century, show part of the town that has changed very little.

THE JUNCTION of Grove Lane and Back Hamlet in 1904.

ARGYLE STREET from Grimwade Street *c*. 1905.

WOODBRIDGE ROAD looking towards Argyle Street *c*. 1905. Samuel Court now stands in place of Singleton the undertaker's building, seen on the left.

CROWDS FILL MAJORS CORNER for an unidentified event *c.* 1910. On the right is the Beehive Inn and the County Hall can be seen in the distance. Nowadays the Odeon Theatre stands in place of the building on the left.

BOTWOODS GARAGE AT MAJORS CORNER was built soon after the First World War. In this 1920s view, one of the town's trams makes its way past the County Hall in St Helens Street. The Odeon Theatre now stands on the left.

UNTIL THE 1960S a car was beyond most families' means, but a motor cycle and sidecar were affordable for many. In this picture of around 1930 Mr Williams of Dickens Road poses with his BSA machine. With him is his nephew.

HOLYWELLS MANSION *c.* 1905. This home of the Cobbold family was built in 1814. Lord Woodbridge purchased the park and mansion in the 1920s and presented it to the town in 1935. Sadly in 1962 the mansion was demolished after falling into disrepair. The stable block, clock tower and conservatory remain.

A FIREPLACE IN THE HOLYWELLS MANSION, lit by magnesium flash powder in this Victorian photograph.

THE ROYAL MAIL SERVICE soon took to using motor vans. The first of the town's motorized mail vehicles, with its oil lamps and solid tyres, stands outside the main post office on the Cornhill in 1907.

LIFEBOAT DAY was a carnival event to raise funds for the lifeboat service. The first was held on 10 July 1897. The new Royal Mail motor van took part in the parade of 1907 and is seen here crossing the Cornhill.

AN AERIAL VIEW of Ransomes Sims and Jefferies Orwell Works in the 1930s. The company's works, which had been on this site since the 1840s, dominate the bottom half of this picture. The photographer was above Duke Street, with Fore Hamlet running from the bottom right corner. The Gardeners Arms public house is in the bottom right corner of the picture. During the 1960s the company moved to their present site on Nacton Road. Between 1965 and 1968 much of the company's workforce had changed their place of work, and the Orwell Works site was sold to the Ipswich Dock Commission. The streets at the top right corner including Woodhouse Street, New Street, East Street, Ernest Street and Regent Street were demolished to clear a site for the Civic (now Suffolk) College and the County Council offices.

DUKE STREET AT 'DINNER TIME' in 1904 as workers pour out of Ransomes Sims and Jefferies Orwell Works. The view is taken from where the Duke Street roundabout is now, with the Anchor Inn on the left and Packard's Chemical Fertilizer works at the Corner of Coprolite Street on the right.

THE PRINCE OF WALES, later the uncrowned King Edward VIII, visited Ipswich on 26 June 1930. He flew into Ipswich Airport from Northholt to perform its official opening. Another of his engagements was a visit to Ransomes Sims and Jefferies where he saw a horse-drawn plough, one of the company's latest lines.

THE PRINCE OF WALES is introduced to directors at the entrance to the plough works of Ransomes Sims and Jefferies by the Mayor Mr A.L. Clouting.

THE TITSHALL BROTHERS toured the town on 26 June 1930 and took pictures of the streets with flags flying for the visit of the Prince of Wales. The pictures on pages 85 to 89 show their work on that special day. Above, Vernon Street from Wherstead Road.

SHOPS IN VERNON STREET, now a block of flats.

VERNON STREET looking towards Stoke Bridge. The Silver Star public house is the only building in this view that remains today.

STOKE STREET from Dock Street. Most of these buildings have since been demolished.

HOUSES IN COLLEGE STREET.

CRANFIELD BROTHERS' MILL and houses with flags flying in Key Street.

THE JUNCTION of Fore Street and Church Street (now Grimwade Street).

LECKENEY'S STORE in St Nicholas House at the corner of Cromwell Street and St Nicholas Street. On the left is the Hippodrome Theatre.

FORE STREET with the Old Neptune Inn on the left, opposite Jackson's chemist shop.

QUEEN MARY made a visit to Ipswich on 14 June 1938. During the day she visited Green and Hatfield's famous antique shop at the corner of St Margarets Plain and Northgate Street.

THE QUEEN CAME TO TOWN in July 1961 to officially open the Civic College (now the Suffolk College). Crowds lined the streets to catch a glimpse of her. Thousands of schoolchildren packed Portman Road football ground together with representatives of local organizations. The Queen toured the ground in an open Land Rover.

CROWDS WAIT FOR THE QUEEN at White Horse corner.

THE QUEEN'S CAR passes from Fore Street to Upper Orwell Street. In the background is Martin and Newby's shop.

THE SUN SHINES ON THE CROWD waiting for the Queen on the Cornhill in July 1961.

THE IPSWICH GAS LIGHT COMPANY was formed in 1821. The company built a gasworks by the River Orwell in 1822 so that it could be supplied with coal by ship. The company stayed in being until it was nationalized in 1948. The picture shows Ipswich Gas Light Company workers in the early 1930s in uniforms made by J. and J. Edwards of Tavern Street. They are, back row, left to right: George Stalley, Herbert Ling, Bert Rymell, Cyril Parker, Ernie Smith, Bill Whybourne, Angus Doyland, Bill Trip, Jock Curtis, Alf Durrant, and Stan Cherry. Second row: Ernie Martin, Walter Kerridge, Bill Ditcham, Johnny Millaird, Jack Jennings, Alf Burrows, Basil Hopes, Bill Green, Bill Gardiner, Harry Crow, Bill Stonham, and Bill Carne. Third row: Frank Tricker, Bill Hardy, Harry Pallant, Nat Mason, Bill Snell, Fred Parker, Alf Miles, George Pinner, B. Cage, Frank Barbrook, Albert Horne, Harry Parker, and A. Hazel. Fourth row: Les Brunning, Bill Lindley, F. Taylor, Bill Jennings, Claude Baker, Alf Fosdyke, Nipper Reynolds, Frank Derrett, Ernie Ranson, Sid Vincent, Jack Johnson, Ted Vanstone, and Albert Clements. Fifth row: Geoff Parker, Herbert Petch, Reg Stollery, Bert Rush, Reg Powell, George Curtis, Ted Jaggs, Reg Mann, Bob Balls, Bills Jackerman, and Bill Emms. Front row: Sammy Bugg, Noel Kindred, Alf Burrows, Dennis Kent, Bill Heath, and Don Burrows.

THE CARR STREET GAS SHOWROOMS shortly before demolition in 1966.

ALL READY FOR CHRISTMAS at Rice's shop on the corner of Tomline Road and Foxhall Road in the early 1930s. Standing proudly with their Christmas fare are Albert and Helen Rice with their children Ethel ('Dickie') on the hand cart, Florence, Olive and Henry. A customer waits by the door in the background while the family poses for the Titshall Brothers.

ISAAC BLOOMFIELD'S BUTCHERS SHOP in Cauldwell Hall Road *c.* 1930, advising customers to order early for Christmas 'to avoid disappointment'.

THE TANKARD INN in Tacket Street in 1948. Now demolished, it once had a colourful reputation.

IPSWICH DOCK was a prime target for the German bombers in the Second World War. The pictures on these two pages show some of the damage caused by bombs. Above, the fuel depot at Cliff Quay and, below, damage to loading equipment at Cliff Quay.

BOMB DAMAGE to warehouses at the dock during the Second World War.

CELEBRATIONS OF PEACE at the Margaret Catchpole in Cliff Lane at the end of the Second World War.

A SPLENDID STEAM LORRY of the Eastern Counties Haulage Company of No. 41 St Nicholas Street. Frank and George King were the proprietors. A picture taken c. 1925.

ALFRED GIBBONS was a miller and corn merchant in Benezet Street. A view of the premises taken in the mid-1920s.

A 1928 PICTURE of Alnesbourne Dairy and Bakeries man Mr Pleasance with his Model T Ford van.

A MILKMAN from the days when milk was delivered by handcart and churn. He appears to be in Levington Road, close to the Alnesbourne Priory Dairy. A picture from around 1910.

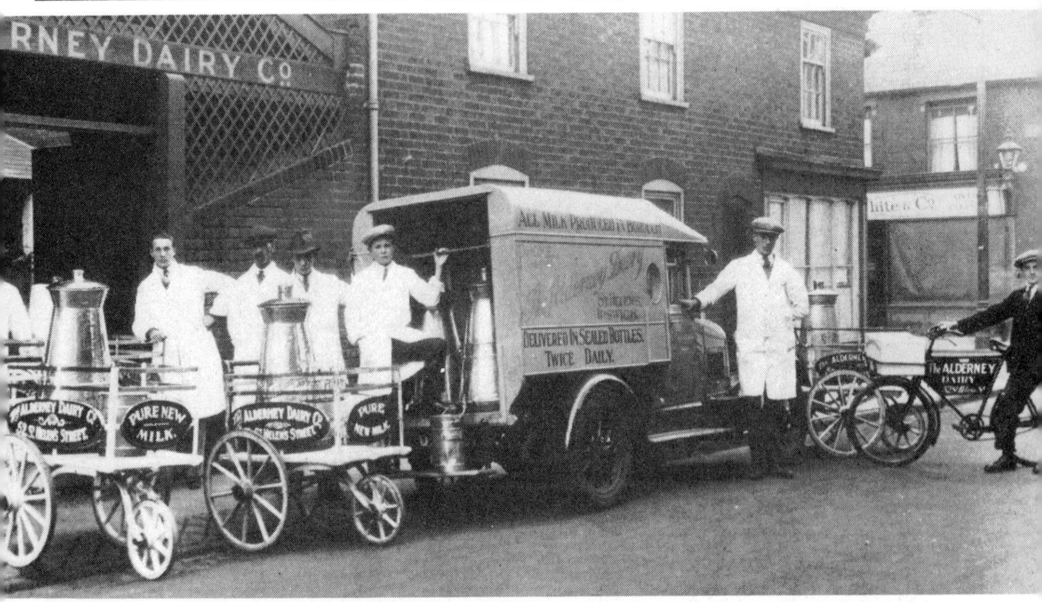

THE ALDERNEY DAIRY STAFF photographed c. 1926 outside their dairy at the junction of St Helens Street and Grimwade Street.

FOUR MILKMEN of Joseph Hunt's dairy line up with their handcarts. Hunt's advertised its milk as being 'under regular medical inspection'. Note their early phone number, 19X.

LOCAL BAKERS included E.C. Catton of Station Street. The van driver was Mr Bert Locksmith (right).

EIGHTEEN-YEAR-OLD MR D.S. SMITH with the van of Yapp and Sons of St Peters Street.

JOSEPH HUNT of No. 331 Spring Road offered 'super bread' and this roundsman holds a loaf with pride as he poses for the camera.

THE BRIDGE OVER THE RIVER ORWELL at Stoke has seen a few changes in its time, and the shape of the bridge itself has altered quite dramatically over the years. Pictures by amateur photographer Ernie Howard, taken on glass plates, show the elegant bridge built in 1818 to replace the stone structure washed away by floods. Mr Howard's picture shows the bridge *c.* 1912. In the background a barge lies alongside the old maltings, used as barracks during the Napoleonic Wars and now converted to flats.

WORK TO REPLACE THE CAST-IRON BRIDGE started on 22 September 1924, the concrete one was completed on 8 April 1925. Buildings close to the bridge were demolished soon after to widen the approach to the bridge.

THE NEWSAGENT'S SHOP at No. 12 Vernon Street, owned by Mrs Bettsie Cutting. A pair of paper boys stand outside in 1906.

BATH STREET with its tramlines leading to Ransomes and Rapier's engineering works. The terraced houses and tramlines are just a memory, as is the name of Ransomes and Rapier, once one of the town's largest employers.

OLD HOUSES IN STOKE STREET in 1899, shortly before they were demolished to make way for the Peoples Hall, which has since been converted to flats and renamed Stoke Hall.

MR SQUIRREL OF SPRING ROAD, known to everybody as 'the greengrocery man' during the late 1920s and early 1930s.

A COALMAN with his horse and cart from Frank Freston's 'general carter and contractor' of No. 42 Princes Street.

THIS BEAUTIFUL VIEW of calm water in Ipswich Dock was taken from Flint Wharf in 1890. Work started on the new dock in 1838. Thirty-three acres of water were enclosed when the lock was shut for the first time on 6 September 1843. A channel, New Cut, was dug to take the water from the river past the dock. Between the sails of the barge on the right is the chimney of Edward Packard's fertilizer works in Coprolite Street. In the centre background is the tower of St Clement's Church.

A HUGE SAILING SHIP, the *Arthur Fidger*, in the lock on 18 April 1900. The picture is by John Gooding.

A STEAM TUG tows an unloaded sailing ship through the lock.

HOT WORK AT FLINT WHARF unloading timber in 1929.

UNLOADING CARGO BY SACK at New Cut in 1929.

LOADED BARGES being towed through the lock in August 1957.

CIGARETTE AND CAP were part of the uniform for bargees. These workers were pictured at Common Quay at the Dock in 1930 by the Titshall Brothers.

A VIEW FROM THE LOCK *c*. 1910. Cliff Quay as we now know it stands as open land with trees on the left. Picture by Ernie Howard.

A VIEW from the opposite direction to the one above, showing children playing by the river. This area was known as Hog Highland before it was developed.

A VIEW OF NEW CUT in 1899. Picture by John Gooding.

ON THE LAND BETWEEN New Cut and the dock there used to be an attractive area of trees, a place popular with townsfolk and visitors, known as the Promenade. An avenue of trees (above) created a peaceful atmosphere. At the lock-gate end was a shelter called 'The Umbrella' (below). These pictures were taken in 1900 by John Gooding.

A PADDLE-STEAMER leaves New Cut and sails down river past The Umbrella in 1894.

THE SS *SUFFOLK* IN NEW CUT. The Great Eastern Railway's paddle-steamer came into service around 1895 and was taken out of service in 1930. The Great Eastern Railway Company ran a service on the Orwell to Harwich and Felixstowe using a trio of paddle steamers. The *Suffolk* was built by Earls of Hull in 1895 and was joined the following year by the *Essex*. The *Norfolk* was built in 1900.

THE STAFF OF FIRMINS SACK FACTORY in Handford Road in the early 1930s.

A PARADE LINES UP for Hospital Sunday *c.* 1916 in Station Street, or Croft Street. The man in the top hat is Mr William Catchpole, a teacher at Smart Street School. A trade union banner is held high as the parade prepares to move off. Not a single head is without a hat for this event.

TWO VIEWS OF UPPER BROOK STREET c. 1908. How long would those glass covers for the gas lamps, hung outside the shops to light the window displays, survive today's vandals?

HORSES WERE USED to shunt trucks around the dock and goods yard in Commercial Road. This rather tired looking pair were photographed at the rail crossing near Stoke Bridge c. 1930.

A VICTORIAN VIEW of houses at the rear of the Ancient House in St Stephens Lane. The clock which projected from St Lawrence Church, in the background, gave the name to Dial Lane.

WORK AT PORTMAN ROAD ATHLETIC GROUND in the early part of the century. The ground was used for many sports events including cricket. The old pavilion was used as the changing rooms and offices of Ipswich Town Football Club until the early 1960s. In the background is the tram depot and power station in Constantine Road. This is now the practice pitch for the club.

ACTION FROM PORTMAN ROAD in the early 1950s with John Elsworthy on the ball. The photographer was at Churchmans end. The crowd in the background are on terracing where the Pioneer Stand is now. The North Stand did not extend to the far corner in those days.

CROWDS PACK THE CORNHILL to celebrate the winning of the Division Two championship by the football club in May 1962.

TOWN PLAYERS ARRIVE on the Cornhill in May 1962 in an open top bus to a huge cheering crowd celebrating the Division Two championship win. Players and officials in the picture include Jimmy Forsyth, Ken Malcolm, John Cobbold, Roy Stephenson, Andy Nelson (captain) with cup, and Larry Carberry.

TWO VIEWS OF ST MARGARETS GREEN, above *c.* 1905, and below in January 1956. The houses on the left of the top picture have been replaced by a garage. A.C. Hardings, builders can be seen on the left of both pictures. In the bottom picture Revetts Motor Cycle shop is on the right.

THE SARACEN'S HEAD public house on St Margarets Green in 1948. This fine old building has been returned to its former style after years as a shop and electrical appliance showroom. It is now a business centre.

STAFF OF SMYTH BROTHERS SHOP in Fore Street c. 1929.

THESE HOUSES AND SHOPS on St Margarets Plain were demolished for redevelopment. Work started to clear the site on 25 February 1936. The shop at the centre of the above picture was Frederick Osborne, bootmaker. The shop that was Green and Hatfield's is on the right of both pictures.

MELLONIE AND GOULDERS LTD COAL MERCHANTS' lorry in Kings Way c. 1930.

A MAGNIFICENT THORNEYCROFT LORRY with solid tyres and gas lamps belonging to Wilfred Christopherson, coal merchant, who had premises in Dial Lane and New Cut West, pictured in the late 1920s.

A VIEW OF THE CORNHILL on 2 February 1957, with trolleybus wires and car parking in front of the Town Hall.

WILSON BATES AND COMPANY of Tacket Street, 'Banana Merchants'. A fine pair of young men with a Thorneycroft lorry in the late 1920s.

LIDBETTERS REMOVALS LORRIES outside their offices in Tanners Lane *c.* 1930. Both pictures on this page by the Titshall Brothers.

THE CENTRAL CINEMA in Princes Street was destroyed by fire in February 1950. In the background is the roof of the Corn Exchange.

FOUNDATION STREET in the 1950s as seen from Tacket Street. All of the buildings left of Terry Neeves camera shop, the corner of which is on the right, have been demolished.

A MULTI-STOREY CAR PARK now stands in place of these old houses in Foundation Street. Though much altered over the years they were substantially the buildings Richard Felaw bequeathed as a school house to Ipswich School in 1483, and known as Felaw's Houses. They were demolished in September 1964.

ST MATTHEWS STREET from Crown Street in 1956. All of the buildings except those on the left are gone. Most went with the redevelopment of the 1960s.

W.J. NICHOLS' BUTCHERS SHOP at the junction of Spring Road. St Helens Street and Grove Lane c. 1910.

THIS RATHER UGLY BUILDING at Majors Corner was demolished in 1969. Many will remember Avis Cook's television shop, Sarony's photographic studio, the Shoe Repair Shop, and Ipswich Travel House. Picture by Terry Neeves.

POSTCARD PHOTOGRAPHERS did not confine themselves to the popular tourist views alone. Backstreet views would sell by the dozen to residents. These two views from around 1915 show Christchurch Street, little changed today, and Milner Street where all of these houses have gone. Somebody at No. 26 has marked their house before sending their message.

SPEEDWAY IS OFFICIALLY RECORDED as first being held in 1923 at West Maitland in Australia, but Ipswich can claim a much earlier advent for oval track motorcycle racing. On 2 July 1904 the local athletic club promoted the Suffolk County Championships followed by motorcycle races. There appears to be nothing in the way of a safety fence for the large crowd at what is now part of the Ipswich Town Football Club ground.

SPEEDWAY HAS LONG BEEN POPULAR in the town. The Ipswich Witches raced their first full season at the new Foxhall Stadium in 1951. This picture of a race start on the original 440 yd track was taken on 22 May 1965. The promotion of Speedway ceased soon after and the track was tarmacked over for stock-car racing. In 1969 promotors John Berry and Joe Thurley started a new era for the sport by building a new track inside the old one.

THE WATERMANS ARMS, a Cobbold pub which was in Foundry Lane *c.* 1927. Landlord Bill Gilbert is at the door.

A 1930S VIEW OF THE CORNHILL from Princes Street.

ST MARGARETS STREET in 1921. Ernest, Ronald and Wilfred Havel are outside their father's shop at No. 18. Mr Havell's was the first gramophone shop in town. He started selling phonographs in 1899, after winning a national competition for the best recordings. His first machine was bought from Edison in America, and he traded directly with Edison Laboratories in the USA. Gramophones gradually replaced phonographs, but Mr Havell was still repairing old cylinder phonographs right up to the end of his business in 1947. He also sold radios, and in the general strike of 1926 a horn loudspeaker was placed outside the shop for people, few of whom had radio, to hear the latest news. Plans to widen the road spelt the end for the business since the shop was under a compulsory purchase order, but it was many years before the shop was demolished. The Odeon Theatre extension now stands on the site.

THE CROSSROADS of Felixstowe Road, Derby Road and Hatfield Road c. 1910. The tram lines came to an end here outside the Royal Oak (right).

TWO PUBLIC HOUSES SINCE DEMOLISHED: the Mitre Tavern in St Helens Street, and the Zulu in Wolsey Street.

THREE IPSWICH SWIMMING PLACES that no longer exist. Stoke Bathing Place (above) was a fenced-off part of the Orwell and home of the Ipswich Swimming Club. The remains of this rather bleak bathing place did not disappear until the building of the West Bank Terminal in the early 1970s. Pipers Vale (opposite page, top) was on the bank of the Orwell near the Gainsborough housing estate. A charming place on a sunny day, as seen in this photograph by Mr W.C.S. Girling in 1952, but like the North Pole when an east wind came up the Orwell. Many people will remember attending swimming lessons as school children, given by teachers dressed in overcoats and gloves. The Orwell Bridge would be in the background today. St Matthews Baths (opposite, bottom) served both as a hall in winter, with the pool covered, as well as the main indoor pool until Crown Pools opened.

THE PUBLIC HALL built in 1868 in Westgate Street was badly damaged by fire in 1948. The organ came from Exeter Hall, London, in 1907 and this too was lost in the blaze.

AN OUTING from the Old Times public house in Cauldwell Hall Road in around 1912 was a great adventure. Were they going to Felixstowe, I wonder?

SHAKESPEARE HOUSE in Falcon Street c. 1935. Demolition work had started in order to clear the site for Cowells printing works, also now demolished, at the corner of Market Lane. Photograph W.C.S. Girling.

ELM STREET in the winter snow of 1956.

MR A. EADE outside his shop at No. 238 Nacton Road with a young customer c. 1928.

THIS CHIMNEY SWEEP of No. 18 Tavern Street, must have been a better sweep than he was a sign writer!

SACKER'S SCRAP MERCHANTS' LORRY at the dock c. 1930.

A HUGE REMOVAL LORRY of H.C. Day Haulage Contractors at No. 961 Woodbridge Road, photographed in Henley Road by the Titshall Brothers c. 1930.

THOUSANDS ONCE WORKED in the Ipswich clothing factory of Phillips and Piper. This picture, of the largely female staff, was taken on 20 December 1963. The building has now been converted to flats.

A GROUP OF DUSTMEN and their dust-cart DX 2144, made by Ransomes Sims and Jefferies, which was one of their range of electric lorries. This is a typical picture by the Titshall Brothers, who did so much to record Ipswich's social history with their pictures of working life.

ANOTHER GROUP OF DUSTMEN and their cart in Lower Brook Street, with Bill Harrison (left), an Ipswich Town Player in the 1923/24 season. With him is Bill 'Dusty' Heffer, Mr Minns, and Mr Dunfirmin.

THE GEORGE ABBOTT CROWN IRON WORKS at the corner of High Street and Crown Street on 16 October 1963 shortly before demolition. The offices of Commercial Union are now on this site.

PEEL STREET, 11 November 1965. Charles Street car park is here now, and offices face Crown Street. In the background is the William Pretty factory.

FORE STREET, 18 July 1961. The buildings on the left were demolished in a road scheme which has since been built on again. Fore Street Baths first opened on 10 March 1894.

A VIEW FROM THE AIR of 14 June 1966, when the redevelopment of the town centre was in full swing. In the foreground work is well advanced on the Greyfriars scheme; work has recently started on the first of the Guardian Royal Exchange buildings (centre left); and the spiral car park is nearing completion. The new Civic Centre, and police station are only just above ground level.

A VIEW OF THE TOWN CENTRE from over St Helens Street in 1964. At the centre bottom of the picture is the junction of Carr Street and Old Foundry Road. The Crown Pools site was then occupied by Egertons Garage. The houses in Fitzroy Street, Charles Street, Beck Street, Chenery Street and Peel Street (top right) were demolished and Crown House and Charles

Street car park now stand there. Tower Ramparts School in the centre of the picture is now Tower Ramparts Shopping Centre. In Carr Street is the tower of the *East Anglian Daily Times* office and printing works. The showrooms and workshops of Eastern Gas ran from Carr Street to Old Foundry Road, where the Eastgate Shopping Centre is now.

TWO PICTURES of Crown Street in 1968, taken by Terry Neeves, provide a near-complete panoramic view. Everything from St Matthews Street on the left to High Street has gone, including the Victorian church at the corner of High Street, built in 1865 and demolished in 1972. Hyde Park House now stands on this corner.

W. J. COE LTD
SALES
LEYLAND
SERVICE
SOLD
GARROD TURNER

ST MATTHEWS STREET was much changed by the developments of the 1960s. Above, a 1920s view looking towards Barrack Corner, and below, the opposite view in the 1950s, with the old Queen's Head public house in the centre. On the left is the entrance to Berners Street. The St Matthews Street roundabout is now on the spot where this picture was taken, with Civic Drive off to the right.

ST MATTHEWS STREET from Hyde Park Corner on 4 December 1963. All the buildings on the right, including the Rainbow public house, were demolished in the mid-1960s road-widening scheme.

BY SEPTEMBER 1963 demolition of the seventeenth-century Golden Fleece Hotel has already taken place (left). Wiggins chemist's shop, with the blind down, stands at the corner of Berners Street.

A VIEW FROM GREYFRIARS TOWER early in 1965 as Civic Drive is cut through from Princes Street.

IT IS JANUARY 1965 and the Greyfriars tower is growing daily. Waiting for demolition are Latimer's Garage and Spurling's saleyard in the foreground, and the terraced houses in Portman Street behind.

A view from the Greyfriars development of the area now occupied by insurance company Willis Faber. In the foreground is the old Grimwade Ridley warehouse. The buildings on the opposite side of Princes Street are much the same today.

ACKNOWLEDGEMENTS

This book is a tribute to the photographers who worked in Ipswich with large wooden field cameras in the early days of photography, making their own wet plates at the scene in a portable darkroom, and also to those working with later equipment that was nevertheless a long way from today's 'idiot proof' cameras.

Many thanks to those over the past few years who have helped me gather the old images: Ralph Chinery, who gave me his father Percy's work from his days in the Ipswich and District Photographic Society in the 1930s; Mr W.C.S. Girling, another member of the society, who loaned me his negatives from the 1930s; Doug Cotton of Camberley Road, Ipswich for access to the wonderful work of the Titshall Brothers; Colin Barber, Derrick Neave, Mike Burrows, Eric Ward, and Edward Storey for pictures from their postcard collections; for Terry Neeves' endless interest in vintage photography and his pictures; and to my late father Noel, who was a member of the Ipswich Photographic Society in the 1930s, and who showed me, when I was a pupil at Landseer Secondary School, how to develop and print films in the cupboard under the stairs at our family home in Cliff Lane.

Thanks also to the *Evening Star's* 'Way We Were' file for so many of the caption details, supplied by the readers of this ever popular feature, and to former *East Anglian Daily Times* colleague Bob Malster for his wonderful book, *Ipswich, A Town on the Orwell*, a gold-mine of information.